Learning about Cats

THE SIAMESE CAT

by Joanne Mattern

Consultant:
Tonja Pfister, Managing Director
Texas Siamese Rescue Organization, Inc.
West Member, Siamese Rescue Alliance

CAPSTONE BOOKS
an imprint of Capstone Press
Mankato, Minnesota

Capstone Books are published by Capstone Press
151 Good Counsel Drive, P.O. Box 669, Mankato, Minnesota 56002
http://www.capstone-press.com

Library of Congress Cataloging-in-Publication Data
Mattern, Joanne, 1963–
    The Siamese Cat/by Joanne Mattern.
    p. cm.—(Learning about cats)
    Includes bibliographical references (p. 45) and index.
    Summary: Discusses the history, development, habits, and care of Siamese cats.
    ISBN 0-7368-0567-2
    I. Siamese cat—Juvenile literature. [1. Siamese cat. 2. Cats. 3. Pets.] I. Title.
II. Series.

SF449.S5 M38 2001
636.8'25—dc21

J
636.825
Matt

00-025407

Editorial Credits
Connie R. Colwell, editor; Linda Clavel, cover designer and illustrator;
    Katy Kudela, photo researcher

Photo Credits
International Stock/Tetsu Yamazaki, 16
Norvia Behling, 4, 6, 8, 18, 22, 24, 26, 33, 34, 36, 39, 40–41
Pallas Photo/Corey Kopischke, 15
Photophile/Roger Holden, cover
Photri Microstock/Prenzel Photo, 20
Pictor, 12; Pictor/Gretchen Palmer, 30
Unicorn/Marshal Prescott, 10; Chris Boylan, 28

Table of Contents

Quick Facts about the Siamese

Description

Size: Siamese cats have long, slender bodies. They are medium-sized cats.

Weight: Male Siamese usually weigh between 8 and 10 pounds (3.6 and 4.5 kilograms). Females usually weigh between 5 and 7 pounds (2.3 and 3.2 kilograms).

Physical features: Siamese cats have short, silky coats. They often have long, triangular heads. All Siamese cats have blue eyes.

Colors: Siamese cats have light-colored to dark-colored coats. The fur on their ears, face, tail, and feet always is darker than their coats. These dark areas are called points.

Development

Place of origin: Most people think that Siamese cats originally came from Siam. This region of Asia is now the country of Thailand. They were known in Thailand as far back as the 1500s.

History of breed: British officials first brought Siamese cats to Europe in the 1800s. These cats soon became popular throughout Europe and North America.

Numbers: In 1999, the Cat Fanciers' Association (CFA) registered 2,389 Siamese cats. Owners who register their Siamese record the cats' breeding records with an official club. The CFA is the world's largest organization of cat breeders.

Chapter 1

The Siamese Cat

Siamese cats are one of the best-known cat breeds. People enjoy Siamese cats for many reasons. Siamese are friendly, intelligent, and attractive cats. They often make excellent pets.

Appearance
Siamese are medium-sized cats. Males usually weigh from 8 to 10 pounds (3.6 to 4.5 kilograms). Females weigh from 5 to 7 pounds (2.3 to 3.2 kilograms). Siamese cats' bodies are long, slender, and muscular.

Siamese cats' coats have an unusual color pattern. Siamese cats have short, solid-colored fur. Their fur also has colorpoints. These dark areas are located on the cats' ears, face, tail, and feet.

All Siamese cats have blue eyes.

Blue-point Siamese have blue-white coats with dark blue points.

Siamese cats have four common coat colors. Seal-point Siamese have light or dark brown coats with dark brown or almost black points. Chocolate-point Siamese have cream-colored coats with dark brown points. Blue-point Siamese have blue-white coats with dark blue points. The blue in blue-point Siamese is blue-gray. Lilac-point Siamese have off-white coats with gray points.

All Siamese kittens are born with white fur. Siamese cats' permanent color patterns and points develop when they are about one year old.

Personality

Siamese cats have friendly personalities. They seem to enjoy being around people and other animals. Siamese often make good pets for families with children, dogs, or other cats.

Siamese cats do not do well alone. They often seem unhappy without people or other animals to interact with. Siamese owners who are not at home for long periods of time may want to adopt another cat. The two cats will be company for each other while the owners are away.

Siamese cats often bond closely with one person. This person usually is the one who feeds the cat. The cat may prefer this person to all others.

Siamese cats are playful and intelligent. They seem to like games such as chasing and fetching balls or toys. Some can learn to do tricks. They often can be trained to walk on a leash.

Siamese are vocal. They often meow loudly to people as if they are talking to them.

Chapter 2

Development of the Breed

People do not know exactly where the Siamese breed began. Siamese cats get their name from the eastern Asian region of Siam. Today, this country is called Thailand.

In the 1500s, Siamese cats were sacred to the Siamese people. These people believed that owning these cats brought good luck. Many people believe that Siamese cats lived as pets in Buddhist temples. Buddhists follow the teachings of Buddha. The cats warned Buddhist priests of strangers. Many people also believe that Siamese cats lived with the king of Siam during this time.

Legend from the Past

The Siamese of the past often had kinked tails and crossed eyes. These features no longer are

Many people believe that Siamese cats lived as pets in Buddhist temples.

Siamese cats may have acted as guards in Buddhist temples.

common in Siamese cats. One of the most popular legends about Siamese cats describes how Siamese got these features. Long ago, two Siamese cats named Tien and Chula lived with a monk in a Buddhist temple. The monk was in charge of guarding a sacred cup.

One day, the monk disappeared. Tien went in search of a new monk to work in the temple. Chula stayed in the temple to guard the sacred cup.

Chula watched the cup for many days and nights. She began to grow tired. She decided to hook her tail around the cup so she could sleep. She knew that no one could take the cup from under her tail without waking her.

Tien returned with a new monk to work in the temple. He found Chula still guarding the cup. But Chula's eyes were crossed from watching the cup for so many days. Her tail was kinked from holding the cup. She also had given birth to kittens. The kittens had crossed eyes and kinked tails like Chula.

Early Siamese History

Siamese cats were important members of Siam's royal court. Some Siamese cats were placed in the tombs of dead kings. Workers dug a hole in each tomb so the cat could escape. When the cat came out, people believed the king's soul was inside the cat.

The sacred cat became part of the royal court. Its job was to watch over the new king. When the cat died, people believed it carried the dead king's soul into the heavens. As recently as 1926, a Siamese cat was part of the coronation of the

new king of Siam. New kings are crowned
during coronations.

The Siamese in Europe and North America
Officials from the British government came to
Siam in the late 1800s. They had never seen a cat
like the Siamese. Many British travelers brought
Siamese cats home with them. At first, many
Europeans thought these cats were strange and
ugly. But some people wanted to own these
unusual cats.

In 1884, the king of Siam gave two Siamese
cats to a British official. The cats were named Pho
and Mia. Pho and Mia became popular in Great
Britain. In 1885, Pho and Mia had kittens. The
kittens won prizes at the 1885 Crystal Palace Cat
Show in London.

In 1878, Rutherford B. Hayes was president
of the United States. Hayes's wife received a
Siamese cat named Siam as a gift. The cat
became sick and died a few months later. But
Siam created great interest in the Siamese breed
in the United States.

Early Siamese Characteristics
The first Siamese cats that came from Siam were
seal-point Siamese. These cats later produced

Seal-point and chocolate-point are common colors for Siamese cats.

chocolate-point, blue-point, and lilac-point kittens. These four colors still exist today.

Siamese cats of the 1800s looked different than today's Siamese. Early Siamese had round heads and small ears. Their bodies were sturdier than the bodies of today's Siamese cats. Early Siamese also had kinked tails and crossed eyes. Past breeders desired Siamese cats with these qualities. Breeders thought these features were true to the Siamese cat's royal background.

Chapter 3

Today's Siamese

Today, Siamese cats look different from those of the past. Some Siamese cats no longer have round heads. Their heads are shaped like a wedge or a triangle. Some of today's Siamese have larger ears than Siamese cats of the past. They also have longer, more slender bodies. Siamese cats with kinked tails or crossed eyes are less common. These traits often are considered defects.

Some people still breed Siamese cats with round heads and sturdy bodies. These cats are called traditional or applehead Siamese. These cats cannot compete in some cat shows.

Many of today's Siamese cats have wedge-shaped heads.

Lynx-point Siamese have striped points.

Coat Colors and Points

The four original colors of Siamese cats are
called classic Siamese colors. These colors
occur naturally in Siamese cats.

Breeders later mated Siamese cats with cats
of other breeds. These cats and the Siamese
produced kittens with various coat colors.
Today, Siamese cats can have a variety of coat
colors and patterns. Some of these include red
or flame point, cream, tabby or lynx point, and

tortoiseshell. Tabbies have faintly striped coats and heavily striped points. Tortoiseshells have points that resemble tortoise shells. These coats consist of patches of black, red, and cream.

In North America, the Siamese breed standard does not include colors other than the four classic colors. Siamese cats with red, cream, lynx, or tortoiseshell coats are classified as a separate breed. These cats are called Colorpoint Shorthairs.

Genes are parts of cells that are passed from parents to their offspring. Genes determine how the offspring will look.

A special gene in Siamese cats causes them to have colorpoints. This gene is heat-sensitive. Cool parts of the Siamese body have dark fur. Warm parts of the Siamese body have lighter fur. All animals with this special gene are born with white coats. The cooler parts of Siamese kittens' bodies turn dark when they are between 4 months and 1 year old. Fur on other parts of the body may turn darker as the cat grows older. This happens because blood does not circulate

as well in older animals. Parts of their bodies become cooler with age.

Breed Standard

Judges look for certain physical features when they judge Siamese cats in cat shows. These features are called the breed standard.

The breed standard says Siamese cats should have long, slender bodies. Their muscles should be firm. Their tails should be long and thin. Their short, shiny coats should lie close to their bodies. The lighter-colored fur on the cat's body should contrast strongly with the dark fur of its points. Points must be seal, chocolate, blue, or lilac.

Today's breed standard does not include traditional, classic, or applehead Siamese. Siamese cats' heads should be shaped like a wedge. Their ears should be large and pointed at the tips. The ears should be in a straight line with the jawline. Siamese eyes should be almond-shaped and slanted toward the nose.

All Siamese kittens are born with white coats.

Chapter 4

Owning a Siamese

People can adopt Siamese cats in several ways. They can buy them from breeders or pet stores. People also may adopt Siamese from animal or breed rescue organizations. Breeders or pet stores may sell Siamese for several hundred dollars or more. Animal or breed rescue organizations can be less expensive places to adopt Siamese cats.

Siamese Breeders

People who want a show-quality Siamese should buy one from a breeder. These people carefully breed their cats to make sure they are healthy. People who buy a kitten from a breeder often can meet the kitten's parents. This gives owners an idea of how the kitten will look and behave as an adult.

A good place to adopt a Siamese cat is from a breeder.

Animal shelters may have Siamese cats available for adoption.

Many Siamese breeders live in the United States and Canada. People who want to find a local Siamese breeder can attend cat shows. Cat shows are good places to talk to cat breeders and see their cats.

Breeders also advertise in newspapers and cat magazines. These ads are organized by breed. They list the names, addresses, and phone numbers of breeders. Some breeders have Internet sites. People should check breeders' references and get the medical history of the breeders' cats.

Pet Stores

People also can buy Siamese cats at pet stores. Pet stores may have Siamese cats available or may be able to get them from a local breeder.

Many pet stores are clean and sell healthy animals. But people should check out a store before they buy a pet from it. Buyers should visit the store and ask store workers where they get their animals. Buyers should look closely at the animals to make sure the animals look healthy and alert. The animals' cages should be large, clean, and comfortable. The animals should have plenty of food, fresh water, and toys. People should not buy cats from pet stores that do not have the animals' medical records available.

Animal Shelters

Many people adopt cats from animal shelters. These places keep unwanted animals and try to find homes for them.

An animal shelter can be a good place to adopt a cat for several reasons. Many people adopt from shelters because they believe they are saving animals' lives. Many more animals are brought to shelters than there are people

Shelters often have mixed-breed pets available for adoption instead of purebred animals like Siamese.

available to adopt them. Animals that are not adopted often are euthanized. Shelter workers euthanize animals by injecting them with substances that stop their breathing or heartbeat.

Animal shelters also offer less expensive pets. Most charge only a small fee. Some veterinarians may provide discounts on medical services for shelter animals.

Shelters do have some disadvantages. Shelters often have mixed-breed pets available for adoption instead of purebred animals such as the Siamese. People can contact a shelter. They can ask shelter workers to contact them if a Siamese cat is brought to the shelter.

Another difficulty with shelter animals is that their histories often are unknown. Shelter workers may not know anything about the shelter animals' parents, health, or behavior. Some owners may adopt cats with medical or behavioral problems.

Many good pets are available at animal shelters. Adopting from a shelter is a good choice for people who do not plan to breed or show their Siamese cats. Shelter animals seldom have papers showing that they are registered with an official cat club. Owners who do not have papers for their cats cannot exhibit them in cat shows.

Breed rescue organizations may have Siamese cats for adoption.

Breed Rescue Organizations

People interested in adopting a purebred Siamese cat may want to contact a breed rescue organization. Breed rescue organization members find unwanted or neglected animals. They care for the animals and try to find new owners to adopt them.

Breed rescue organizations are similar to animal shelters in many ways. But they usually rescue just one breed. They rarely euthanize the animals. Rescue organizations keep Siamese cats until people are available to adopt them.

Adopting a Siamese from a breed rescue organization can have some advantages over adopting from breeders and animal shelters. Breed rescue organizations are less expensive than breeders. People may find a purebred Siamese for a small fee. These cats may even be registered.

People can find information about breed rescue organizations in several ways. These organizations often have their own Internet sites. They also may advertise in newspapers or cat magazines. Animal shelters also may refer people to breed rescue organizations.

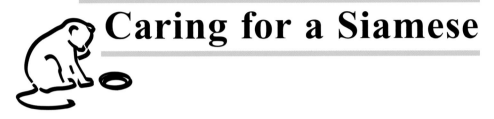

Chapter 5

Caring for a Siamese

Siamese are strong, healthy cats. They can live 15 years or more with good care.

Indoor and Outdoor Cats

Some cat owners allow their cats to roam outdoors. This practice is not safe. Cats that roam outdoors have a much greater risk of developing diseases than cats that are kept indoors. Outdoor cats also face dangers from cars and from other animals.

Owners of indoor cats need to provide their cats with a litter box. Owners fill the box with small bits of clay called litter. Cats eliminate waste in litter boxes. Owners should clean the waste out of the box each day and change the litter often. Cats are clean animals. They may refuse to use a dirty litter box.

Cats that roam outdoors have a much greater risk of developing diseases than cats that are kept indoors.

Both indoor and outdoor cats need to scratch. Cats mark their territories by leaving their scent on objects they scratch. Cats also scratch to release tension and keep their claws sharp. This habit can be a problem if cats choose to scratch on furniture, carpet, or curtains. Owners should provide their cats with scratching posts. Owners can buy scratching posts at pet stores. They also can make them from wood and carpet.

Feeding

Siamese cats need high-quality food. Most pet foods in supermarkets or pet stores provide a balanced, healthy diet.

Some owners feed their cats dry food. This food usually is less expensive than other types of food. Dry food also can help keep cats' teeth clean. It will not spoil if it is left in a dish.

Other owners prefer to feed their cats moist, canned food. This type of food should not be left out for more than an hour. It will spoil if it is left out for long periods of time. Owners who feed their cats moist food usually feed their adult cats twice a day. The amount of food needed depends on the individual cat.

Siamese cats need high-quality cat food.

Both types of food can be suitable for Siamese cats. Different cats may prefer different types of food. Owners can ask a veterinarian for advice on which type of food is best for their cats.

Cats need to drink fluids to stay healthy. Owners should keep their cats' bowls filled with fresh, clean water. Owners should dump and refill water bowls twice a day.

Most cats do a good job of grooming their fur with their tongues.

Grooming

Most cats do a good job of grooming their fur with their tongues. Siamese coats are sleek and easy to care for. Siamese require only an occasional brushing to remove loose hair. Owners may rub their cats' coats with a damp, soft cloth to keep the coats shiny and clean.

The tip of a cat's claw is called the nail. Siamese cats need their nails trimmed every few weeks. Trimming helps reduce damage if cats scratch the carpet or furniture. It also protects cats from infections caused by ingrown nails. Infections can occur when a cat does not sharpen its claws often. The claws then grow into the pad or bottom of the paw.

It is best to begin trimming a cat's nails when it is a kitten. The kitten will become used to having its nails trimmed as it grows older. Veterinarians can show owners how to trim their cats' nails with a special nail clipper.

Dental Care

Siamese cats also need regular dental care to protect their teeth and gums from plaque. This coating of bacteria and saliva causes tooth decay and gum disease. Dry cat food helps remove plaque from cats' teeth. Owners also should brush their cats' teeth at least once a week. They can use a special toothbrush made for cats or a soft cloth. They should use a toothpaste made for cats. Owners should never use toothpaste made for people. Cats may become sick if they swallow it.

Many veterinarians recommend that owners begin brushing their cats' teeth when the cats are kittens.

Brushing may not be enough to remove the plaque from older cats' teeth. These cats may need to have their teeth cleaned once each year by a veterinarian.

Health Problems

Siamese cats have no specific health problems. They sometimes are born with crossed eyes.

These cats cannot compete in cat shows. But crossed eyes do not affect a cat's health.

Cats sometimes get diseases that are passed down from their parents. Good cat breeders test their animals for these diseases. They will not breed animals that suffer from serious illnesses. Breeders should have information on their cats' medical histories. This information is important when choosing a Siamese cat.

Veterinarian Visits

Siamese cats must visit a veterinarian regularly for checkups. Most veterinarians recommend yearly visits for cats. Older cats may need to visit the veterinarian two or three times a year. More frequent checkups will help the veterinarian spot health problems in older cats.

An owner who adopts a Siamese cat should make a checkup appointment as soon as possible. The veterinarian will check the cat's heart, lungs, internal organs, eyes, ears, mouth, and coat.

The veterinarian also will give vaccinations to the Siamese. These shots of medicine help prevent serious diseases. These diseases include rabies, feline panleukopenia, and feline leukemia.

Rabies is a deadly disease that is spread by animal bites. Most states and provinces have laws that require owners to vaccinate their cats against rabies. Feline panleukopenia also is called feline distemper. This disease causes fever, vomiting, and death. Owners who travel to shows often vaccinate their cats for feline leukemia. This disease attacks a cat's immune system. It leaves the cat unable to fight off infections and other illnesses. Feline leukemia is spread from cat to cat by bodily fluids. Cats also can be vaccinated against several respiratory diseases that cause breathing or lung problems.

Cats should receive some vaccinations each year. Some are given less often. Breeders have information on which vaccinations Siamese cats need. Owners should keep a record of their cats' vaccination dates. This record helps owners make sure that their cats have received all the vaccinations that they need.

Veterinarians also spay female cats and neuter male cats. These surgeries make it impossible for cats to breed. Owners who are not planning to breed their cats should have them spayed or neutered. The surgeries keep unwanted kittens

Siamese cats can live 15 years or longer with proper care.

from being born. They also help prevent diseases such as infections and cancers of the reproductive organs. Spayed and neutered cats usually have calmer personalities than cats that are not spayed or neutered. They also are less likely to wander away from home to find mates.

Regular visits to the veterinarian are an important part of cat ownership. Owners and veterinarians can work together to help Siamese cats live long, healthy lives.

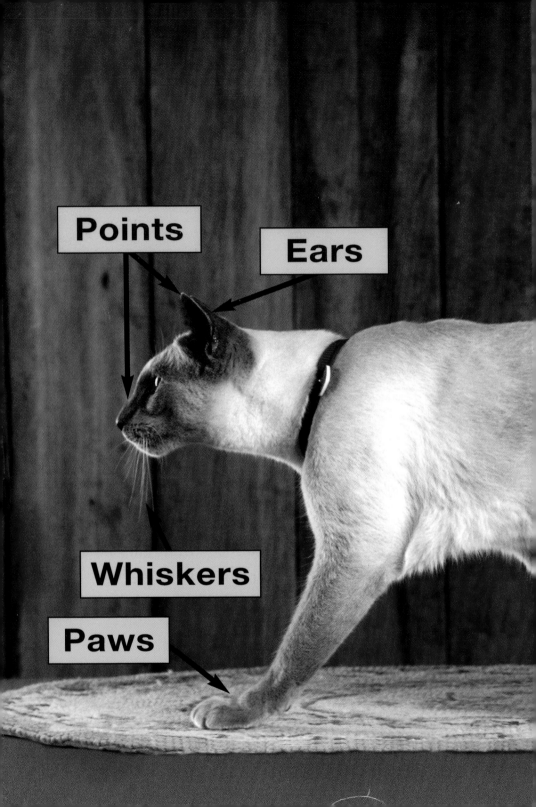

Points

Ears

Whiskers

Paws

Tail

Points

Points

Quick Facts about Cats

A male cat is called a tom. A female cat is called a queen. A young cat is called a kitten. A family of kittens born at one time is called a litter.

Origin: Shorthaired cat breeds descended from a type of African wildcat called *Felis lybica*. Longhaired breeds may have descended from Asian wildcats. People domesticated or tamed these breeds as early as 1500 B.C.

Types: About 40 domestic cat breeds exist. The Cat Fanciers' Association recognizes 33 of these breeds. The smallest breeds weigh from 5 to 7 pounds (2.3 to 3.2 kilograms) when grown. The largest breeds can weigh more than 18 pounds (8.2 kilograms). Cat breeds may be either shorthaired or longhaired. Cats' coats can be a variety of colors. These colors include many shades of white, black, gray, brown, and red.

Reproduction: Most cats mature at 9 or 10 months. A sexually mature female cat goes into estrus several times each year. Estrus also is called "heat." During this time, she can mate with a male. Kittens are born about 65 days after breeding. An average litter includes four kittens.

Development: Kittens are born blind and deaf. Their eyes open about 10 days after birth. Their hearing develops at the same time. They can live on their own when they are 6 weeks old.

Life span: With good care, cats can live 15 or more years.

Sight: A cat's eyesight is adapted for hunting. Cats are good judges of distance. They see movement more easily than detail. Cats also have excellent night vision.

Hearing: Cats can hear sounds that are too high for humans to hear. A cat can turn its ears to focus on different sounds.

Smell: A cat has an excellent sense of smell. Cats use scents to establish their territories. Cats scratch or rub the sides of their faces against objects. These actions release a scent from glands between their toes or in their skin.

Taste: Cats cannot taste as many foods as people can. For example, cats are not very sensitive to sweet tastes.

Touch: Cats' whiskers are sensitive to touch. Cats use their whiskers to touch objects and sense changes in their surroundings.

Balance: Cats have an excellent sense of balance. They use their tails to help keep their balance. Cats can walk on narrow objects without falling. They usually can right themselves and land on their feet during falls from short distances.

Communication: Cats use many sounds to communicate with people and other animals. They may meow when hungry or hiss when afraid. Cats also purr. Scientists do not know exactly what causes cats to make this sound. Cats often purr when they are relaxed. But they also may purr when they are sick or in pain.

Words to Know

breeder (BREED-ur)—someone who breeds and raises cats or other animals

breed standard (BREED STAN-durd)—specific physical features that judges look for in a breed at a cat show

estrus (ESS-truss)—a physical state of a female cat during which she will mate with a male cat; estrus also is known as "heat."

euthanize (YOO-thuh-nize)—to painlessly put an animal to death by injecting it with a substance that stops its breathing or heartbeat

neuter (NOO-tur)—to remove a male animal's testicles so it cannot reproduce

spay (SPAY)—to remove a female animal's uterus and ovaries so it cannot reproduce

tabby (TAB-ee)—a cat with a striped coat

vaccination (vak-suh-NAY-shuhn)—a shot of medicine that protects an animal from disease

veterinarian (vet-ur-uh-NER-ee-uhn)—a doctor who is trained to treat the illnesses and injuries of animals

To Learn More

Alderton, David. *Cats.* Eyewitness Handbooks. New York: DK Publishing, 1992.

Collier, Marjorie McCann. *Siamese Cats: Everything about Acquisition, Care, Nutrition, Behavior, Health Care, and Breeding.* Hauppauge, N.Y.: Barron's, 1991.

Kallen, Stuart A. *Siamese Cats.* Checkerboard Animal Library. Edina, Minn.: Abdo & Daughters, 1996.

Stone, Lynn M. *Siamese Cats.* Read All about Cats. Vero Beach, Fla.: Rourke, 1999.

Yule, Brenda. *Guide to Owning a Siamese Cat.* Popular Cat Library. Philadelphia: Chelsea House, 1999.

You can read articles about Siamese cats in *Cat Fancy* and *Cats* magazines.

Useful Addresses

Canadian Cat Association (CCA)
220 Advance Boulevard
Suite 101
Brampton, ON L6T 4J5
Canada

Cat Fanciers' Association (CFA)
P.O. Box 1005
Manasquan, NJ 08736

The International Cat Association (TICA)
P.O. Box 2684
Harlingen, TX 78551

Siamese Rescue Alliance—West
606 Swan Drive
P.O. Box 3088
Coppell, TX 75019

The Traditional Cat Association
18509 NE 279th Street
Battle Ground, WA 98604-9717

Internet Sites

American Veterinary Medical Association Presents—Care for Pets
http://www.avma.org/care4pets

Canadian Cat Association (CCA)
http://www.cca-afc.com

Cat Fanciers' Association (CFA)
http://www.cfainc.org

Rescue Siamese and Stray Cats
http://www.geocities.com/Heartland/Meadows/6430/rescue.html

Siamese Internet Cat Club
http://www.meezer.com

Siamese Rescue Alliance
http://www.siameserescue.org

Index